My Dog's Seeing Eye Dog

ISBN 979-8-89526-217-7 (paperback)
ISBN 979-8-89526-218-4 (digital)

Christian Faith Publishing
832 Park Avenue
Meadville, PA 16335
www.christianfaithpublishing.com

Illustrated by Holly Chignola

Printed in the United States of America

My Dog's Seeing Eye Dog

Laura Chignola

Illustrated by Holly Chignola

It was adoption day! Today I would find my new owners. As the first family came in, my brothers and sisters pushed to get to the front of the circular pen. I was the smallest of them all. One by one, I saw my brothers and sisters get picked. At the end of the day, it was just me, alone. I was very sad, but then I heard a car door shut and footsteps coming my way.

As they opened the door to come into the house, a shy little girl walked in with her parents. She came toward me slowly, and I did the same. I was so scared they would not want me, just like everyone else. She put her hand in the pen, and I licked it. She giggled, and I wagged my tail. She said to her mommy and daddy, "This is the one I waited for." Funny, because I realized she was the one I was waiting for too.

We headed home. Now, I had never been in a car before, so it was scary for me. But the little girl held me tight, making me feel safe. I was all black with a little white butterfly shape on my chest. They decided to name me Chester. Chester—what a great name! My new family was ready for me. They bought me all kinds of fun toys to play with. They took me to the backyard, where I had so much room to play and run around. There was even a trail leading into the woods! They had two cats; I made friends with them, but they didn't enjoy playing with me.

I would go for walks in the woods with my new family. I walked my girl to the bus stop and watched her get on the big yellow metal thing. It was bigger than a car, and I had never seen anything like it before. It scared me at first. I thought it was taking her away, and it made me sad and worried.

Later in the afternoon, Mommy walked me down the street, and we waited at the same place the big yellow thing had been. I saw it again; it came toward us, and I hid behind Mommy's legs. Just then, I saw Sissy get off what I learned was called a bus. She was back! The bus didn't eat her.

I loved my new family. We played all the time, and I had so much fun when Sissy's friends came over. Then winter came. I saw snow for the first time and did not know what it was. Daddy shoveled a path for me in the backyard because I was too little. I couldn't jump over the tall snow. Winter was a little boring because I couldn't go for my walks in the woods as much. I had to wait for the snow to melt so my little legs could walk in it.

As winter dragged on, I became very lonely during the day. Sissy would be at school, and Mommy and Daddy would be at work. Every time I heard a car, I knew it was Mommy coming home so we could take our walk to get Sissy off the bus. At least that's what I heard Mommy say.

Spring finally came. I didn't grow as tall as I had hoped. Actually, I didn't really grow much at all, but I felt bigger. One day, I heard Mommy and Daddy talking about getting another dog to keep me company. *What?* I didn't think I wanted another dog. What if my family loved them more than me?

One day, we all went for a ride in the car. I stuck my head out the window, feeling the nice, warm air of spring on my face. We pulled up to my favorite store. It always had amazing toys and treats for me. I was so excited to get some more toys! Then we walked into the store, and I saw so many puppies, dogs, kittens, and cats. *Is this a party for pets?* I wondered. Nope, we were there to adopt another dog.

Sissy asked Mommy, "How will we know which one to pick?"

Mommy said, "We are not picking them. Chester is."

Me? Well, okay.

I went from puppy to puppy. *Nope, not this one. This one is too loud. This one is too frisky.* Then I saw him. He was hiding in the back of his pen, just like I did, waiting to be adopted. Did he have brothers and sisters that were picked before him too?

When I went up to the pen, he was afraid. I heard the lady telling Mommy and Daddy that his name was Sammy. He came from a bad home, so he was afraid of loud noises and had a scar on his ear. He was six months old but the same size as me! I barked, letting him know it was okay. He came over to me, and both of our tails started wagging. Yep, this was my new brother, and I was going to take good care of him.

We took Sammy home, where I showed him the backyard and the trails in the woods. He looked so happy, like this was a whole new world to him.

As time went on, Sammy grew and grew and grew! I was still small, but it didn't bother me. We were the kings of the woods. We never had to be put on a leash, and we were allowed to run and explore. We always knew when it was time to get back on the trail by Daddy whistling or Mommy calling for us. Sammy and I were best friends. I showed him the ropes from the beginning.

One day, I started to get sick. After a few weeks, Mommy took me to the doctor. The doctor gave me some medicine and told Mommy I had to stay on this medication, or I would become sick again. I didn't mind. They would wrap my pill in some cheese…*Yum!*

A few more years went by, and one day, we were taking our daily walk in the woods. I got separated from Sammy, and I got confused. Everything went blurry. I called out to Sammy. *Bark! Bark! Bark!* I saw a big sandy shape coming my way. I did not know what it was, but as it got closer and closer, I realized it was Sammy! He knew I was scared, and he walked with me until we were on the trail again, by Mommy and Daddy.

A few more weeks went by, and Mommy noticed I was banging into things more often. I was scared; everything was blurry all the time. She took me to the doctor again. He had helped me last time, so I thought he could just give me another medication to make the blurriness go away! But the doctor said I was losing my eyesight and going blind. I didn't know what that meant, but it didn't sound good because Mommy started crying. She took me home, and I just lay in my bed. The doctor could not fix this.

Sammy kept wanting to play, but I wasn't in the mood. Then the day finally came; I woke up and couldn't see anything.

I started barking and barking and barking. I was so scared. Sammy came right to my side and started licking me to comfort me. Sissy ran over to me. I couldn't see her! When she called my name, I tilted my face toward the sound but couldn't see her. I guess this is what Mommy was crying about; she knew what was going to happen to me but couldn't tell me.

I was blind. I didn't know what to do, so I just closed my eyes and lay there. I lay there for a long time. The days passed, and Sammy never left my side. Sissy would give me my medicine and pet me to let me know she was there. Mommy let me cuddle with her on the couch and bed so I would feel safe. Sammy slept at the bottom of the bed every night too.

Because I couldn't see, Daddy would take Sammy for a walk in the woods without me—our woods, without me. I would cry out for Sammy each time, but I went on my own walks with Mommy on a leash up and down the street so I wouldn't hurt myself. I enjoyed my walks with Mommy, but I missed our walks in the woods.

Then one day, Mommy took me on the leash, but we didn't go down the street. I could feel we were at the entrance to our trail in the woods.

Mommy kept me on a leash, and I cried out for Sammy. *Bark! Bark! Bark!* I could hear Sammy running to me once he saw me. He was licking me and getting excited. He was barking and barking. I knew he was telling Mommy to take my leash off, but she did not understand dog talk. Finally, she took off the leash; and Sammy, right by my side, guided me through the woods, making sure I stayed on the trail. I knew the smells of the woods by heart. I knew where I was, even though I couldn't see it. If I got too close to a tree, Sammy would nudge me the other way. He stayed right by my side, and I followed him.

Wherever I went from that day on, Sammy was there, guiding my steps. My best friend became my Seeing Eye dog.

About the Author

Laura and Holly Chignola are a mother-daughter duo based in North Carolina, both originally from New Jersey. Holly has graduated with a BFA in illustration, while Laura works for a local nonprofit organization. Both love their community and God. They love to serve and touch the hearts of others. This is the first book created together, and they wish to relate more in the future.